WHAT'S IN A POEM?

BOOK TWO

EDITOR: BILL BOYLE

ILLUSTRATIONS BY JONATHAN HILLS

COLLINS EDUCATIONAL

CONTENTS

UNIT 1   GROWING UP

Growing Up   *Gareth Owen*   2
Chivvy   *Michael Rosen*   4
Arithmetic   *Gavin Ewart*   5
Dumb Insolence   *Adrian Mitchell*   6
Nearly Thirteen   *Jan Dean*   7

UNIT 2   SCHOOL

Schoolpoem 2   *Brian McCabe*   9
Slow Reader   *Vicki Feaver*   11
Teachers   *Michael Rosen*   12
A History Lesson *Miroslav Holub*   13
Writing   *Jan Dean*   14
Monday Morning   *Joanne*   14

UNIT 3   OUR ESTATE

Ford Estate   *Joanne*   16
Tower Block   *Michael Rosen*   18
Number 14   *Keith Bosley*   19
Old Birkenhead   *Joanne*   20
Our Estate   *Lindsey*   22

UNIT 4   NIGHT LIFE

City Lights   *Margaret Greaves*   24
Night   *Lindsey*   26
Shadows   *Robbie*   27
November Night, Edinburgh
   Norman MacCaig   27
A City Night   *Robert*   28

UNIT 5   PEOPLE

Proletarian Portrait
   William Carlos Williams   30
The Hunchback in the Park
   Dylan Thomas   32
I Know Someone Who Can. . .
   Joanne   33
The Boxer   *Lynn*   33
Uncle Edward's Affliction
   Vernon Scannell   34

UNIT 6   INSIDE YOURSELF

A Boy's Head   *Miroslav Holub*   36
Street Boy   *Gareth Owen*   38
An Ordinary Day *Norman MacCaig*   39
I Would Like to Paint   *Colin*   40
Curiosity Conversation   *Joanne*   40

UNIT 7   CONVERSATIONS

Rabbiting On   *Kit Wright*   42
Conversations   *Suzanne*   44
Passing Comments *Michael Rosen*   45
Talk   *D H Lawrence*   45
Sergeant Brown's Parrot
   Kit Wright   46

UNIT 8   Feelings

The Man Who Wasn't There
   Brian Lee   48
The Lake   *Roger McGough*   50
I Wonder How Many People in this City
   Leonard Cohen   52
Anger   *Helen*   53
A Death   *Lynn*   54

UNIT 9   THE SENSES

The Apple's Song   *Edwin Morgan*   56
Fish and Chips   *L T Baynton*   58
This is Just to Say
   William Carlos Williams   59
from Blackberry Picking
   Seamus Heaney   60

UNIT 10   OLD AGE

Café Portraits   *Roger McGough*   62
Notes for the Future   *Jim Burns*   64
Home   *Paul Donnelly*   65
Days   *Vicki Feaver*   66

UNIT 11   AT WORK

Father's Gloves   *Ted Walker*   68
Nenthead   *Tom Pickard*   70
Apprentice Worker   *Jackie*   70
Poem for Merseyside
   Robert and Colin   71
The Barber Shop *Charles Reznikoff*   72

UNIT 12   TRAVELLING

Off Course   *Edwin Morgan*   74
Legging the Tunnel
   Gregory Harrison   76
Motorway   *Lindsey*   77
Canal   *Jane*   77
This Subway Station
   Charles Reznikoff   78
Portrait of a Motor Car
   Carl Sandburg   78

UNIT 13   GAMES

I'll Stand the Lot of You *Martin Hall* 80
Northern Line   *Tom Pickard*   82
Cowboy   *Richard Hill*   83
Hide and Seek   *Vernon Scannell*   84

UNIT 14   NATURE

Thistles   *Ted Hughes*   86
Round Pond   *Vicki Feaver*   88
Suburb   *Charles Reznikoff*   88
Child on Top of a Greenhouse
   Theodore Roethke   89
Numbers   *Stevie Smith*   90

UNIT 15   CREATURES

Considering the Snail *Thom Gunn*   92
from The Fly   *Anthony Thwaite*   94
Rookery   *Seamus Heaney*   94
Creatures   *Suzanne*   95
Horses   *Paddy Kinsale*   96

UNIT 16   FISH

Trout   *Seamus Heaney*   98
Four Fish   *Ted Walker*   100
Fish   *Una*   101
Pike   *Karl*   101
Fish   *Ann*   101
Pollution   *Philip*   101
from Pike   *Ted Hughes*   102

UNIT 17   CRUELTY

The Dog Lovers *Spike Milligan*   104
Take One Home for the Kiddies
   Philip Larkin   106
Goldfish   *Alan Jackson*   106
My Mother Saw a Dancing Bear
   Charles Causley   108

UNIT 18   WEATHER

Blue Toboggans   *Edwin Morgan*   110
Wind   *Ted Hughes*   112
Rain   *Norman Nicholson*   113
Winter   *Chris*   114
Rainfall   *Michael*   114
Winter's Day   *James*   114

WHAT'S IN A POEM?

Description   115
Shape   116
Experiences   118
Moods   119
Comparisons   120
Movement   121

PREFACE

This series is designed to introduce children to the enjoyment that can be gained from experiencing poetry. Such initial experiences should be pleasurable, so that the child will want to repeat them, and will want to explore the many forms and styles that come under the broad umbrella of poetry.

Although teaching ideas are included in each unit, they are not intended to be rigidly followed. Poetry 'lessons' depend for their success upon a sympathetic relationship between teacher and pupils. It is hoped that these ideas will provide starting points for the teacher and child to begin a creative exploration of poetry together.

Many of the poems in the book have been written by children. Their names are shown in italic type.

Bill Boyle
1983

Collection copyright © Bill Boyle 1983

First published 1983, Reprinted 1984, 1985, 1987, 1988

Photoset in 11/12½ point Optima and 13/13 point Bembo by GMGraphics, Harrow-on-the-Hill, Middlesex.

Printed and bound in Britain by Bell and Bain Ltd, Glasgow.

ISBN 00 314831 9

UNIT 1

GROWING UP

GROWING UP

I know a lad called Billy
Who goes along with me
He plays this game
Where he uses my name
And makes people think that he's me.

Don't ever mess with Billy
He's a vicious sort of bloke
He'll give you a clout
For saying nowt
And thump you for a joke.

My family can't stand Billy
Can't bear him round the place
He won't eat his food
He's always rude
And wears scowls all over his face.

No one can ever break Billy
He's got this look in his eye
That seems to say
You can whale me all day
But you'll not make Billy cry.

He has a crazy face has Billy
Eyes that look but can't see
A mouth like a latch
Ears that don't match
And a space where his brains should be.

Mad Billy left one morning
Crept away without being seen
Left his body for me
That fits perfectly
And a calm where his madness had been.

Gareth Owen

What's in this poem?

With your partner, read 'Growing Up', each reading a verse in turn. Who is Billy? Find the lines of the poem in which the writer tells you how Billy behaves. What does the family think of Billy? What difference was there when Billy left?

Look at the last verse of the poem. Why did Billy go? What makes you think the writer was glad that Billy had gone? Talk about the expression 'two sides to your personality' and decide if it fits in with this poem.

Do you think everyone has got *only* two sides to their personality? Discuss your own personality – whether you have different sides to it, and what they are. Have they changed as you have grown up?

Make a list of the different sides to your personality. Describe one incident when one side of your personality took over. What happened? Did it lead to a quarrel with someone? Did you upset someone at home? How did the incident end?
Let each member of the group read their account aloud.

Choose the account (above) that you all find most interesting. Discuss how you could act it through. Perhaps the **action** will change as you work on it. The **dialogue** and the **relationships** between the characters in the account will also change as you dramatise the incident.

Read the other poems in the unit. Pick out the one you like best. Which one best describes you? Which is the most serious poem?

Think about whether life is easier for a child than a grown-up. Why does a child become a grown-up? Consider what being grown-up means. Are you keen to grow up?

Some adults seem to be always criticising youngsters. Why is this? Do you think they understand young people?

Chivvy

Grown-ups say things like:
Speak up
Don't talk with your mouth full
Don't stare
Don't point
Don't pick your nose
Sit up
Say please
Less noise
Shut the door behind you
Don't drag your feet
Haven't you got a hankie?
Take your hands out of your pockets
Pull your socks up
Stand up straight
Say thank you
Don't interrupt
No one thinks you're funny
Take your elbows off the table
Can't you make your own
    mind up about anything?

Michael Rosen

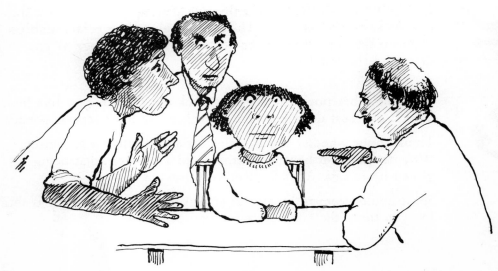

Arithmetic

I'm 11. And I don't really know
my 2 Times Table. Teacher says it's
    disgraceful.
But even if I had the time, I feel too tired.
Ron's 5, Samantha's 3, Carole's 18 months,
and then there's the Baby. I do what's required.

Mum's working. Dad's away. And so
I dress them, give them breakfast. Mrs Russell
moves in, and I take Ron to school.
Miss Eames calls me an old-fashioned word:
    Dunce.
Doreen Maloney says I'm a fool.

After tea, to the Rec. Pram-pushing's slow
but on fine days it's a good place, full
of larky boys. When 6 shows on the clock
I put the kids to bed. I'm free for once.
At about 7 – Mum's key in the lock.

Gavin Ewart

Dumb Insolence

I'm big for ten years old
Maybe that's why they get at me

Teachers, parents, cops
Always getting at me

When they get at me

I don't hit 'em
They can do you for that

I don't swear at 'em
They can do you for that

I stick my hands in my pockets
And stare at them

And while I stare at them
I think about sick

They call it dumb insolence

They don't like it
But they can't do you for it

I've been done before
They say if I get done again

They'll put me in a home
So I do dumb insolence.

Adrian Mitchell

Nearly Thirteen

I'm nearly thirteen and my name isn't Mary,
It's Lola, I'm wild and exotic and mean.
My mum's not my real mum. My mother's a gypsy
And one day she'll claim me and I'll be their queen.

The people I live with don't understand me.
They don't seem to realise I am unique.
I'm going to be famous and sinful and blasé,
As soon as they let me out nights in the week.

I want to wear satin and black fishnet stockings.
I want feather boas and glittering rings.
One eye on the mirror, I practise seductions,
And plan the sensation peroxide will bring.

I want it all now. I want it to happen.
I am Mata Hari and Brigitte Bardot.
All they can think of is cabbage and homework,
When I want a party they always say no.

They think I'm a kid. I fight them. I lose.
God, I wish I had breasts and could wear high-heel shoes.

Jan Dean

UNIT 2
SCHOOL

SCHOOLPOEM 2

One day i went into the school library and
                    there were no books. Panic-stricken
i looked for explanations in the eyes
            of a school-tied librarian but
she just stamped a date on my wrist
                and said i was overdue.
Then i spied one little book called
            How to Spell
                        but
            i new how to do that already,
        so i sat feeling pretty lonely
as you can imagine in a bookless library,
            in the skeleton of a library,
going over all the names of the books i once new:
                War and Peace
                Danny the Dormouse
how nice and neat and safe they were.
        Now all i do is look for answers
                in my blazer pockets but
they have gone through the holes
                made by yesterday's
                        marbles.

Brian McCabe

What's in this poem?

You probably spend a lot of your time in school. Your experiences at school will give many ideas for talking and writing. Brian McCabe's poem takes a thoughtful and amusing look at one incident in school life.

The child's experience was quite frightening. When he went into the school library he was surprised and alarmed. Think of some reasons for this. What did he expect to find in the library? Who did he turn to for help?

Find the clue which tells us how good his spelling is. What does the writer mean by using the phrase 'the skeleton of a library'? Why is the child feeling lonely?

The child gives the titles of two books. If you had to quickly name two books, what would they be? Where have the answers to the child's questions gone?

Do we go to school for answers? Who asks the questions? Talk about the 'answers' the poem mentions. Where do answers come from? Decide whether you think they are all found in books.

Do you think we learn from being with other people?

With your group, work out a sequence around the idea of the books on the shelves watching and discussing the children who come in to the school library. They are looking at the children's movements and actions, and commenting to each other about them.

You are writing your 'Life Story'. Write the chapter about your years spent at school.

What experiences will you remember? Are they good or bad? Why will you remember them? Will you learn from them?

Are you in a group or a gang at school? Describe the other children in your group. Why do you stick together?

Slow Reader

He can make sculptures
And fabulous machines
Invent games, tell jokes
Give solemn adult advice
But he is slow to read.
When I take him on my knee
With his Ladybird book
He gazes into the air
Sighing and shaking his head
Like an old man
Who knows the mountains
Are impassable.

He toys with words
Letting them grow cold
As gristly meat
Until I relent
And let him wriggle free –
A fish returning
To its element
Or a white-eyed colt
Shying from the bit
As if he sees
That if he takes it
In his mouth
He'll never run
Quite free again.

Vicki Feaver

Teachers

Rodge said,
'Teachers – they want it all ways –
You're jumping up and down on a chair
or something
and they grab hold of you and say,
"Would you do that sort of thing in your own home?"

'So you say, "No."
And they say,
"Well don't do it here then."

'But if you say, "Yes, I do it at home."
They say,
"Well, we don't want that sort of thing
going on here
thank you very much."

'Teachers – they get you all ways,'
Rodge said.

Michael Rosen

A History Lesson

Kings
like golden gleams
made with a mirror on the wall.

A non-alcoholic pope,
knights without arms,
arms without knights.

The dead like so many strained noodles,
a pound of those fallen in battle,
two ounces of those who were executed,

several heads
like so many potatoes
shaken into a cap –

Geniuses conceived
by the mating of dates
are soaked up by the ceiling into infinity

to the sound of tinny thunder,
the rumble of bellies,
shouts of hurrah,

empires rise and fall
at a wave of the pointer,
the blood is blotted out –

And only one small boy,
who was not paying the least attention,
will ask
between two victorious wars:

And did it hurt in those days too?

Miroslav Holub

Writing

and then i saw it

saw it all   all the mess

and blood and evrythink

and mam agenst the kichin dor

the flor all stiky

and the wall all wet

and red an dad besid the kichen draw

i saw it saw it all

an wrot it down an ever word of it is tru

You must take care to write in sentences.
Check your spellings and your paragraphs.
Is this finished? It is rather short.
Perhaps next time you will have more to say.

Jan Dean

Monday Morning

How I dread
a Monday morning –
no lying in,
school.

Your aching wrists,
your broken pencils,
and your arguments.

Joanne

FORD ESTATE

Writing on the walls.
Gossip everywhere
One O'Clock Gun,* have you heard about that?
They've driven the old man out.
Smashing windows.
                    You vandals!
Terrible isn't it, it's darn terrible.
My kid fell on the playground the other day.
Mums complaining.
Bonfire night's the worst.
They come round pinching your fences.
Oh! Tommy just got stuck in Ford Towers' lifts.

Now it's night time.
Everyone in bed.
Only the vandals are out.
Writing on walls. Smashing windows.
Ain't it terrible!
Now I've got to wash Tommy John's pants.
He fell over on that mud.
I heard they battered an old lady up and took her bread.
Tommy! Come here!
It's terrible.
Our Peter fell on the playground today.
Have you seen Herondale Avenue?
My auntie got robbed when she went on holiday.
Our John's just fell over a brick,
And the baby's got knocked over by a skateboard.
We haven't even got a park.
Have you seen all the paint on the walls,
Windows smashed and everything?

Joanne

*The pub on the Estate. Local
youngsters forced the old publican to
leave after he enforced the ban on
drinking for those under 18.

What's in this poem?

Joanne's poem gives us a very good idea of what life's like on her estate. She uses things she has seen and heard on the estate to build up her **word picture.**

Read the poem again and list the events Joanne mentions. Then look back at the photograph at the beginning of the section, which may give you more details about estate life to add to your list.

In her poem Joanne uses several words and phrases more than once. Find them. The reason why she repeats 'It's terrible' is because that's what people are always saying. Write down any **catch phrases** you hear around you.

Now make your own word picture of where you live. Describe only things you have seen or heard people talking about.

Discuss the **mood** or **tone** of Joanne's poem. Is it serious or light-hearted? Do you feel she likes living on the estate? Do other people like living on the estate? Perhaps the poem is enjoyable because she mixes serious events with less serious ones. Can you find examples of this? When you come to read the other poems in this section, try to think about these things. Which poem seems most serious?

Divide into small groups and pretend you are neighbours gossiping about your estate. Imagine that something bad/good/surprising has just happened. Try and use some of the catch phrases you thought of.

Tower Block

Think of this tower-block
as if it was a street standing up
and instead of toing and froing
in buses and cars
you go up and down it
in a high speed lift.

There will be no pavement artists of course
because there aren't any pavements.
There isn't room for a market
but then there isn't room for cars.
No cars: no accidents
but don't lean out of the windows
don't play in the lifts
or they won't work.
They don't work
and they won't work
if you play Split Kipper,
Fox and Chickens, Dittyback,
Keek-bogle, Jackerback,
Huckey-buck, Hotchie-pig,
Foggy-plonks, Ching Chang Cholly
or Bunky-Bean Bam-Bye.
Go down. The stairs are outside –
you can't miss them – try not to miss them, please.
No pets.
Think how unhappy they'd be
locked in a tower-block.
There will be
no buskers, no hawkers,
no flowers, no chinwaggers,
no sandwichboards,
no passers-by,
except for
low-flying aircraft
or high-flying pigeons.

Michael Rosen

Number 14

That house you took me to
as a child, with its steps down
from the pavement into a doorway
that smelled of damp, along a passage
into a parlour with a black-leaded grate
and a brace of partridge in white
porcelain, that house
where you grew up under your father's belt –
I pass it every day, and up till now
I have watched the street it stood in
fall to the buldozers, house by house
each day a bit more sky:
oldman, the bulldozers have gone away
but your house is still there
its red front door still saying number 14
its windows hooded with corrugated iron
jagged against the sky; its time come
and gone, waiting for one more stroke.

Keith Bosley

Old Birkenhead

A dirty dark dusk floats comfortably,
Reminding people of their misfortune in wartime,
Reminding people of terror and fear,
Of old and young,
And old Birkenhead and its ways.
Ilchester Square.
Alleyo 123.
You're caught.
                    No, I'm not!
Some playing jacks on the uneven paving stones.
The blocks of flats looked on to an arena
Where children played and fought with each other.
Line up at number 57 for flapjacks,
With penny in hand, from Mrs Brown,
Or borrow a bike off Mrs Burton,
For a penny an hour.
Sometimes, hours of happiness,
Other times, sadness, in this rough area.
This is all gone.
But memories linger on.

The torment of the round arena,
Tapping on windows, pulling tongues,
And then running away,
Tripping over his undone shoe laces.
He pulled up his knee-length shorts
And snorted,
Hitting small children and laughing.
The torment of the street,
He was frightened of no one,
The terror of the Bull Ring.

The old market,
The wind blows on the old shutters,
Once they were used,
Heels clicking on the cobblestone floors.
Once there was an atmosphere.
Once everything there was alive.

Walking around an old building,
Full of buyers and sellers,
The same dirty old smell,
Memories of the past,
As you sit outside on the doorstep,
Dressed in an old-fashioned outfit,
Longing to smell the atmosphere.

Jessie Annie Hudson (1892-1972)
Rub, rub, scrub, scrub, splash, splash,
Washing in the old dolly tub,
Aching arms, through mangling clothes, never stop,
Rubbing the step,
Eating, working and play,
Hanging out the washing with dolly pegs.
Sun shines through the small square windows,
Working all the time.
Mam's work never done.

The Tip.
Concealed in old drums,
Discarded tyres and the wrecks of cars,
Children lounge about over the rubbish;
Nothing to do in their spare time,
Covered in muck and dust they play.
At night, the wasteland is empty,
Only the moonlight shines.

Modern council houses with a cheap structure
Stand gloomily
Leaning to one side.
The green grass once stretched over the fields,
A gate led to each part,
Altogether seven gates.
Now the clean countryside spoilt,
By dirty, crowded houses and factories.
The light blue sky,
Turns to a smoky grey,
Silhouetting the plan of houses for the future.

Joanne

Our Estate

Desolate landscapes, vandals' playground, ghost town,
Chip papers flutter like milky white butterflies.
Pepsi Cola cans roll with a ghostly tune of their own.
Toffee wrappers and muddy chocolates cover the floor
  like a carpet.
Broken glass, glinting sparkles captured star-like.
Mud-streaked skies, dirty grimy corners.
White writing on walls. Windows barred,
Keeping vandals as prisoners.

Lindsey

UNIT 4
NIGHT LIFE

CITY LIGHTS

Huge round oranges of light
Ripen against the thin dark of the city sky,
Spilling their juice in warm pools
   on bare dry pavements.
Below them blink the traffic lights
   like the eyes of enormous cats
Crouching in the dark –
Crouching and breathing with the heavy purr of traffic;
And winking tail lights slide and dart
   like goldfish
In the pale streams pouring from
   shop windows.

Margaret Greaves

What's in this poem?

'City Lights' is a poem describing the streets of a city at night time. Even though the scene is set against the dark background of night, the poem includes many **colourful images.**

What are the 'oranges of light'? How do they 'spill their juice in warm pools'? Find out what the traffic lights are compared to. Why has the writer chosen this image?

How many different kinds of lights are mentioned in the poem?

Why does the writer say that the traffic 'purrs'? What does she mean? What other words would describe the noise of the traffic?

What does the phrase the 'tail lights slide and dart like goldfish' mean?

Many of the shop windows have their lights on. Why is this? What effects do they make on the pavements?

Read the other poems in the unit. Which one is nearest to your experience of night life? Are the descriptions **realistic?**

Look at the photographs at the beginning of the unit and on page 26. List the 'night sights' that you can see. Use **comparisons** (as in 'City Lights') to make your description more effective.

Imagine that you live in the middle of the city or think about your own home, if you do so already. Perhaps you live high in a flat or in a terraced, busy street. Write down what you would see if you looked out at night. Describe the buildings, the street scene, the shapes in the darkness. What sounds do you hear? Are the noises different from daytime? What smells are in the air? Does the moon have any effect upon the scene?

Night

Lamp posts tall, they glow like matches,
Spreading light over vast expanses of dull, grey pavement.

Lindsey

Shadows

Big and long
peeping out of entries.

Robbie

November Night, Edinburgh

The night tinkles like ice in glasses.
Leaves are glued to the pavement with frost.
The brown air fumes at the shop windows,
Tries the door and sidles past.

I gulp down winter raw. The heady
Darkness swirls with tenements.
In a brown fuzz of cotton wool
Lamps fade up crags, die into pits.

Frost in my lungs is harsh as leaves
Scraped up on paths. I look up, there,
A high roof sails, at the mast-head
Fluttering a grey and ragged star.

The world's a bear shrugged in his den.
It's snug and close in the snoring night.
And outside like chrysanthemums
The fog unfolds its bitter scent.

Norman MacCaig

A City Night

As I gaze at the houses,
from the balcony of our flat,
the moonlit scene reveals small crevices
in corners of walls.

I come out from the coop of our room
for a breath of fresh air in my lungs,
the stale smell of cigarette smoke dies
in the breeze. As I look at the shops,
'Joe's' is just closing. The posters of 'Kiss'
are peeling away from the poster-board.
Graffiti has taken over the Hemmeling advert.
The fish-and-chip stand is closed for the night,
leaving a strong scent of vinegar in the air.

The street lamps suddenly die out, and the persistent
noise of traffic stops, as time reaches to midnight.
The clock chimes. Wire mesh thuds as shop windows
are bashed by passing yobboes. The wire makes
an eerie noise in the night air.

The dark creepy alley way is a black shadow
in the scenery. The teenagers torment a tramp sleeping
on a park bench. Then all you can hear is a slow muttering
that becomes quieter until dawn.

Robert

UNIT 5
PEOPLE

PROLETARIAN PORTRAIT

A big young bareheaded woman
in an apron

Her hair slicked back standing
on the street

One stockinged foot toeing
the sidewalk*

Her shoe in her hand. Looking
intently into it

She pulls out the paper insole
to find the nail

That has been hurting her.

William Carlos Williams

*pavement

What's in this poem?

This poem is short and looks very simple. However, it contains a lot of information. It describes a woman's **appearance** clearly, and gives the details of her **actions.**

What are you told about the woman? Is she small or big? Is she wearing a hat? What style is her hair worn in? Find the other details you are told about the woman in the poem.

How does the poet describe what the woman is doing? What **action words** are used?

There is one sentence for each separate action. Why do you think the poem is set out like this?

Does the writer tell you what was the reason for the woman's action? Is this a good moment in the poem to give you this information?

Look at the photograph on the page before the poem. Try to describe the woman as accurately as you can. Look at her face, her mouth, her hands. Note down what you see. Describe her clothes. Can you describe her feelings from studying the photograph?

Write your description carefully, giving all the information that you think your reader will need. Do not waste words. Use only those that are **working** to complete the picture of the woman.

Observe your family, friends, people you meet. Practise keeping **details** in your mind. Jot down short descriptions.

You have just witnessed a robbery. Give a short but accurate description to help the police identify the robbers.

With a partner, hold a conversation in which you talk about a third person. Give as much detail as you can, but do not name him/her. See how long it takes your friend to guess who you are describing.

from **The Hunchback in the Park**

The hunchback in the park
A solitary mister
Propped between trees and water
From the opening of the garden lock
That lets the trees and water enter
Until the Sunday sombre bell at dark.

Eating bread from a newspaper
Drinking water from the chained cup
That the children filled with gravel
In the fountain basin where I sailed my ship
Slept at night in a dog kennel
But nobody chained him up.

Like the park birds he came early
Like the water he sat down
And Mister they called Hey Mister
The truant boys from the town
Running when he heard them clearly
On out of sound

Past lake and rockery
Laughing when he shook his paper
Hunchback in mockery
Through the loud zoo of the willow groves
Dodging the park keeper
With his stick that picked up leaves.

Dylan Thomas

I Know Someone Who Can . . .

I know someone who can put a piece of paper
   in his nose and make it come out of his mouth,
I know someone who can put a pipe in his ear
   and puff smoke out of his nose,
I know someone who can wrap paper round a comb,
   and play a tune by mouth,
I know someone who can eat an egg with the shell on it,
   and make the shell come out of his ear,
I know someone who can complete the Rubic Cube
   in less than ten seconds,
I know someone who can walk into a lamp post,
   and say, 'Oops! Sorry.'
I know someone who can put his right hand behind
   his back,
and tie his shoe laces with his left hand,
And,
I know someone who can eat
THREE SHREDDED WHEAT!

Joanne

The Boxer

He punches the bag with furious rage
   and deadly accuracy.
Sweating but carrying on determinedly,
he snatches a glance at the ring.
One day he will be up there.
Neon lights glowing through smoky,
   unbreathable air.
One day he will be up there, fighting,
battling for survival.

Lynn

33

Uncle Edward's Affliction

Uncle Edward was colour-blind;
We grew accustomed to the fact.
When he asked someone to hand him
The green book from the window-seat
And we observed its bright red cover
Either apathy or tact
Stifled comment. We passed it over.
Much later, I began to wonder
What a curious world he wandered in,
Down streets where pea-green pillar boxes
Grinned at a fire-engine as green;
How Uncle Edward's sky at dawn
And sunset flooded marshy green.
Did he ken John Peel with coat so green
And Robin Hood in Lincoln red?
On country walks avoid being stung
By nettles hot as a witch's tongue?
What meals he savoured with his eyes:
Green strawberries and fresh red peas,
Green beef and greener burgundy.
All unscientific, so it seems:
His world was not at all like that,
So those who claim to know have said.
Yet, I believe, in war-smashed France
He must have crawled from neutral mud
To lie in pastures dark and red
And seen, appalled, on every blade
The rain of innocent green blood.

Vernon Scannell

UNIT 6
INSIDE YOURSELF

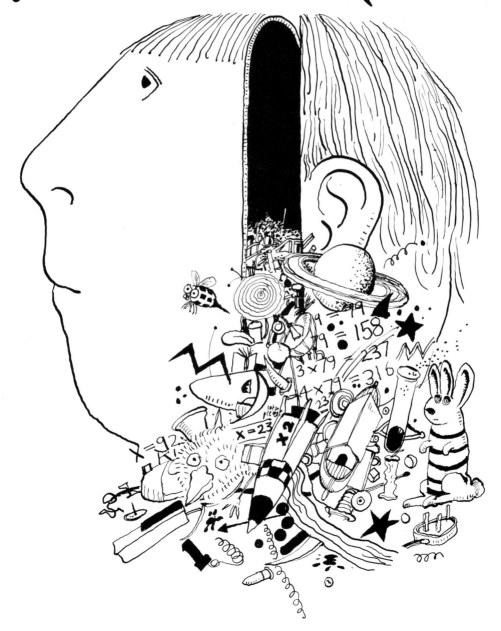

A BOY'S HEAD

In it there is a space-ship
and a project
for doing away with piano lessons.

And there is
Noah's ark,
which shall be first.

And there is
an entirely new bird,
an entirely new hare,
an entirely new bumble-bee.

There is a river
that flows upwards.

There is a multiplication table.

There is anti-matter.

And it just cannot be trimmed.

I believe
that only what cannot be trimmed
is a head.

There is much promise
in the circumstance
that so many people have heads.

Miroslav Holub

What's in this poem?

We all have our own thoughts, our dreams and our projects. Miroslav Holub's poem explores some of these ideas that are spinning around inside a boy's head.

How many different ideas and plans are mentioned in the poem? What are the new inventions that the boy has in mind? What use would the multiplication table be? Does the boy like piano lessons? What is he interested in?

What does the writer mean by 'cannot be trimmed'? Why is the fact that a head 'cannot be trimmed' a good thing? What does Holub think shows 'much promise'? Talk about what you think he means by this.

Read 'Street Boy' by Gareth Owen on page 38. What does the street boy say his head is full of? Does he have ambitions? What are they? How would anyone know about them?

What thoughts are spinning around your head? What inventions or projects would you like to work on? What ambitions do you have for your life? What are you thinking about at the moment? Re-write Holub's poem in your own way, under the title 'A Girl's Head'.

Read 'An Ordinary Day' by Norman MacCaig. How many ordinary things have happened today? Let your imagination turn them into extraordinary happenings. As we all have 'heads', our reactions to our experiences will always be individual. With this in mind, write your own version of an 'Ordinary Day'.

Street Boy

Just you look at me, man,
Stompin' down the street
My crombie stuffed with biceps
My boots is filled with feet.

Just you hark to me, man,
When they call us out
My head is full of silence
My mouth is full of shout.

Just you watch me move, man,
Steady like a clock
My heart is spaced on blue beat
My soul is stoned on rock.

Just you read my name, man,
Writ for all to see
The wall is red with stories
The streets is filled with me.

Gareth Owen

An Ordinary Day

I took my mind a walk
Or my mind took me a walk –
Whichever was the truth of it.

The light glittered on the water
Or the water glittered in the light.
Cormorants stood on a tidal rock

With their wings spread out,
Stopping no traffic. Various ducks
Shilly-shallied here and there

On the shilly-shallying water.
An occasional gull yelped. Small flowers
Were doing their level best

To bring to their kerb bees like
Aerial charabancs. Long weeds in the clear
Water did Eastern dances, unregarded

By shoals of darning needles. A cow
Started a moo but thought
Better of it . . . And my feet took me home

And my mind observed to me,
Or I to it, how ordinary
Extraordinary things are or

How extraordinary ordinary
Things are, like the nature of the mind
And the process of observing.

Norman MacCaig

I would like to paint . . .

I would like to paint the stars and show them to the moon
and sun and make them upset.
I would like to paint the waves of the sea and let them
sail away and not return.
I would like to paint a swan and make it fly.
I would like to paint a mind of my own.
I would like to paint with a squirrel's tail or the whisker
of a mouse.
I would like to paint a swallow and put it on a roof.
I would like to paint the sky and show it to the crashing
waves.
I would like to paint myself and show it to a grave.
I would like to paint a wooden ruler to show to a plastic
ruler.
I would like to paint the world and show it to the
Martians.

Colin

Curiosity Conversation

Who are you?   Me
What are you?   Me
How are you?   Myself
Where are you?   The inside of outside.

I am the same Me as You,
inside of outside.
        I'm bored.

Joanne

UNIT 7
CONVERSATIONS

RABBITING ON

Where did you go?
Oh . . . nowhere much.

What did you see?
Oh . . . rabbits and such.

Rabbits? What else?
Oh . . . a rabbit hutch.

What sort of rabbits?
What sort? Oh . . . small.

What sort of hutch?
Just a hutch, that's all.

But what did it look like?
Like a rabbit hutch.

Well, what was in it?
Small rabbits and such.

I worried about you
While you were gone.

Why don't you stop
Rabbiting on?

Kit Wright

What's in this poem?

Kit Wright's poem records a **conversation** between two people. One asks the questions, while another supplies the answers. The questions and answers make a regular **pattern**, like a poem.

Look out also for the **rhymes**, and the **play on words** at the end of the poem.

Notice where the poem rhymes. Is it a rhyming pattern? Read the poem aloud with a partner, one reading the questions, another providing the answers. Who do you think are the two people talking in the poem? Is the conversation getting anywhere? Are you getting much information from the answers in the poem?

Do you find the poem funny? Is it a serious conversation? What is 'clever' about the ending? Do you like words being used like this?

Listen to conversations at home and at school. What do you discover? Is Kit Wright's poem a typical conversation? How often do you hear people saying things just for the sake of saying something? What is a 'red herring'? Talk about whether many of the conversations you hear reach an ending. Do some go off in strange directions?

Listen out for **expressions** like 'you know' and 'and such'. These often appear in conversations. List others you hear.

Think of situations when you might be asked questions, like those in 'Rabbiting On'. Perhaps your mother has asked you where you have been. Work out how the conversation would go. Keep to a pattern of question and answer. Try to reach an ending, whether it is serious or amusing.

Read your conversation aloud with your partner. You may need to change it after you have heard it read out to make it sound better.

Jokes have a similar pattern. Make up a 'knock knock' type of joke to read out.

Conversation

'Look, Henry, that number 26 is washing her step again.
I wouldn't mind if she washed her house as well.
Hey up, here comes Curly.
I'm sure she wears them curlers all day, every day.
Hey, Freddy, shout our Tom to keep off the road.
There's number 49 talking to her next door.
Bet she's talking about us.
She is, she's pointing over here.
That's all they do here. Talk about other people's business.
Number 57's doing her washing in the window as usual.
That newcomer looks clean, but the kids don't.
They've got muck ground into them.
Henry, I hope you're listening to me!
There she goes again pointing at us.
Henry, get over there, sort her out!
Do you hear me? Get over there, you coward!'

Suzanne

Passing Comments

Some people
are always passing comments.
They say to me:
hallo hairy
your hands are huge
do you know your eyes pop out?
you're a monster
you aren't half white
your fingers are like sausages
you walk like a bear
is that thing on your chin a wart?

Michael Rosen

Talk

I wish people when you sit near them,
wouldn't think it necessary to make conversation
and send thin draughts of words
blowing down your neck and your ears
and giving you a cold in your inside.

D H Lawrence

Sergeant Brown's Parrot

Many policemen wear upon their shoulders
cunning little radios. To pass away the time,
They talk about the traffic to them, listen to the news,
And it helps them to Keep Down Crime.

But Sergeant Brown, he wears upon his shoulder
A tall green parrot as he's walking up and down
And all the parrot says is 'Who's a-pretty-boy-then?'
'I am', says Sergeant Brown.

Kit Wright

UNIT 8

FEELINGS

THE MAN WHO WASN'T THERE

Yesterday upon the stair
I met a man who wasn't there;
He wasn't there again today,
I wish, I wish, he'd go away.

I've seen his shapeless shadow-coat
Beneath the stairway, hanging about;
And outside, muffled in a cloak
The same colour as the dark;

I've seen him in a black, black suit
Shaking under the broken light;
I've seen him swim across the floor
And disappear beneath the door;

And once, I almost heard his breath
Behind me, running up the path:
Inside, he leant against the wall,
And turned. . . and was no one at all.

Yesterday upon the stair
I met a man who wasn't there;
He wasn't there again today,
I wish, I wish, he'd go away.

Brian Lee

What's in this poem?

'The Man Who Wasn't There' is a poem about **feelings.**
Particularly, the feelings of fear and loneliness that many children
have when they are on their own in the dark.

What has frightened the child in the poem? What does he think he
has seen? What does the child think he once heard? Pick out the
lines in the poem which build up this feeling of fear.

What has the child really seen? Find the clues in the poem which
tell you about the identity of the 'man'. How would he 'swim
across the floor'? Whose breath had the child heard?

Talk about what you think makes people frightened in the dark.
Do you go upstairs alone in the dark? Do you ever imagine that
you see things? What do you think causes this?

Describe any fears you may have about the dark. Are there any
dark corners in your house that frighten you? What do you
imagine is lurking there? Make your writing as scary and as sinister
as possible.

Possible starting points could be: exploring an old house at night,
walking through a thick dark wood, or going down a dark, unlit
alleyway.

Read 'The Man Who Wasn't There' aloud, making it sound as
frightening as you can. With your group, act out the scene that the
poet describes. How will you show the shadows? Make the
breathing as sinister as you can.

Try out ways of combining the actions and the words.

The Lake

For years there have been no fish in the lake.
People hurrying through the park avoid it
like the plague. Birds steer clear
and the sedge of course has withered.
Trees lean away from it,
and at night it reflects, not the moon,
but the blackness of its own depths.
There are no fish in the lake,
But there is life there. There is life . . .

Underwater pigs glide between reefs of coral debris.
They love it here. They breed and multiply
in sties hollowed out of the mud
and lined with mattresses and bedsprings.
They live on dead fish and rotting things,
drowned pets, plastic and assorted excreta.
Rusty cans they like the best.
Holding them in webbed trotters
their teeth tear easily through the tin,
and poking in a snout, they noisily suck out
the putrid matter within.

There are no fish in the lake.
But there is life there. There is life . . .

For on certain evenings after dark
shoals of pigs surface
and look out at those houses near the park.
Where, in bathrooms,
children feed stale bread to plastic ducks,
and in attics,
toy yachts have long since run aground.
Where, in living rooms,
anglers dangle their lines on patterned carpets,
and bemoan the fate of the ones that got away.

Down on the lake, piggy eyes glisten.
They have acquired a taste for flesh.
They are licking their lips. Listen . . .

Roger McGough

I Wonder How Many People in this City

I wonder how many people in this city
live in furnished rooms.
Late at night when I look out at the buildings
I swear I see a face in every window
looking back at me,
and when I turn away
I wonder how many go back to their desks
and write this down.

Leonard Cohen

Anger

Your blood is like boiling water, ready to erupt.
Your face is like a beetroot, red with anger.
Your hands are clenched, the muscles tight.
You walk around heavily with a long face.
Someone asks you a question, and you ignore them.
You get really hot and sweaty.

'Upstairs,' says Mum.
'You go to bed and cool down.'

Helen

A Death

Black armbands worn with tight intensity.
Silence lines the streets,
laughter falls into the gutter.
No one dares speak.
One minute of utter silence seems like an hour.
A patriot, our hero.
Now he is dead.

Lynn

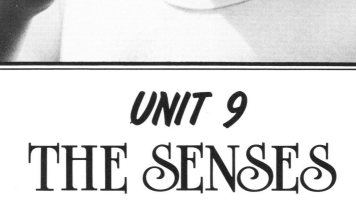

UNIT 9
THE SENSES

THE APPLE'S SONG

Tap me with your finger,
rub me with your sleeve,
hold me, sniff me, peel me,
curling round and round
till I burst out cold and white
from my tight red coat
and tingle in your palm
as if I'd melt and breathe
a living pomander
waiting for the minute
of joy when you lift me
to your mouth and crush me
and in taste and fragrance
I race through your head
in my dizzy dissolve.

I sit in the bowl
in my cool corner
and watch you as you pass
smoothing your apron.
Are you thirsty yet?
My eyes are shining.

Edwin Morgan

What's in this poem?

We rely on our five **senses** to give us the information that we need about our surroundings. 'The Apple's Song' by Edwin Morgan shows the senses working together. Which senses come into the poem? Find as many **touch** words as you can. What words does the writer use to make you almost **taste** the apple? Pick out any words that give the **scent** of the apple. What does the apple **look** like? Find the word that describes the **feel** of the apple.

Talk about the ways in which we rely on our senses. What are the important jobs that they do?

Which is the most necessary sense? Imagine being without one of your senses. How do you think you would be affected?

Make a list of the sounds that you like and dislike. Shut your eyes. Listen. Now write down all the sounds you heard.

Describe the special sounds and smells of: the seaside; a fairground; a football crowd; the zoo; a fish and chip shop.

Choose a colour that you like, and use that colour in a poem which gives as many **images** describing the colour as possible.

Make up your own advertising jingle to describe your favourite food. Be sure that it appeals to the taste buds of your audience. It must make their mouth water so that they want to go out and buy it!

Read 'This is Just to Say' on page 59. Leave your own message describing what you have just eaten and how it tasted.

Fish and Chips

Heading for the light, bitter cold night,
Round this corner – smell it now?
Windows steamed like fog inside.
Hungry queue all bags in hands.
Old papers piled but not to read,
Giant sized salt and vinegar near,
And wooden forks like babies' toys.
Nearer now, oh hear the hiss,
And on the shelf the golden plaice, the chips.
At last my turn, my mouth is wet –
No thanks, not wrapped – hot in my hand.
Outside the night seems warmer now,
Until – I hold a crumpled paper ball
Why do they go so soon?

L T Baynton

This is Just to Say

I have eaten
the plums
that were in
the icebox

and which
you were probably
saving
for breakfast.

Forgive me
they were delicious
so sweet
and so cold.

William Carlos Williams

from **Blackberry-picking**

Late August, given heavy rain and sun
for a full week, the blackberries would ripen.
At first, just one, a glossy purple clot
Among others, red, green, hard as a knot.
You ate that first one and its flesh was sweet
Like thickened wine: summer's blood was in it
Leaving stains upon the tongue and lust for
Picking. Then red ones inked up and that hunger
Sent us out with milk-cans, pea-tins, jam-pots
Where briars scratched and wet grass bleached our boots.
Round hayfields, cornfields and potato-drills
We trekked and picked until the cans were full,
Until the tinkling bottom had been covered
With green ones, and on top big dark blobs burned
Like a plate of eyes. Our hands were peppered
With thorn pricks, our palms sticky as Bluebeard's.

Seamus Heaney

UNIT 10
OLD AGE

From
CAFÉ PORTRAITS

A pair of pensioners nibble
at their cups of tea
their mouths saying old-fashioned things
(for their minds are many miles ago)
one twirling the sugarbowl
with bony fingers
the other drawing daydreams
in the spilt milk.

Roger McGough

What's in this poem?

Roger McGough has watched a couple of elderly people sitting together in a café. He has looked at them carefully and recorded their actions accurately.

What word does the writer use to describe how the old couple drink their tea? What other uses can you think of for this word?

What kind of 'old-fashioned' things do you think the people might be saying? What is meant by the phrase 'their minds are many miles ago'?

Do we respect older people or just dismiss them as 'past it'? Discuss whether you think young people should respect their elders more.

How do people **change** as they become older? Think of some problems the old might face. How are old people usually shown on television or in the newspapers?

What do you hope for 'when you're sixty-four'?

Build up your own imaginary conversation between two old people. They could be meeting in the street; sitting in a café; visiting one another's home. What would they be talking about? How would their conversation develop? Would it jump from subject to subject? Would sentences fade away? Use snippets of actual conversation you have heard to make your writing more real.

Compile a diary of a day in the life of a pensioner. Include their **feelings** and **thoughts** as they notice the changes all around them.

Act out a situation where two old people are together. Use your **observations** of old people to help you copy their actions and mannerisms.

Tape your grandparents and other old people in the neighbourhood talking about their childhood, schooldays and memories.

Notes for the Future

When I get old
don't dress me in
frayed jackets
and too-short trousers,
and send me out
to sit around bowling-greens
in summer.
Don't give me just enough
to exist on, and expect me
to like passing
the winter days
in the reading-room
of the local library, waiting
my turn to read
last night's local paper.
Shoot me!
Find a reason, any reason,
say I'm a troublemaker
or can't take care of myself
and live in a dirty room.
If you're afraid
of justifying my execution
on those terms,
tell everyone I leer
at little girls, and then
shoot me!
I don't care why you do it,
but do it,
and don't leave me
to walk to corner shops
counting my coppers,
or give me a pass to travel cheap
at certain times, like a leper.

Jim Burns

Home

in streets I once knew
the moon is trapped in an attic
and the net of stars is frozen
over an old house

an old man
rattles the fire's remains
in a shadowy room
smoking he draws his chair
to the black grate
sees streets he once knew
hears a child call his name.

Paul Donnelly

Days

They come to us
Empty but not clean –
Like unrinsed bottles

Sides clouded
With a film
Of yesterday.

We can't keep them.
Our task is to fill up
And return.

There are no wages.
The reward is said to be
The work itself.

And if we question this,
Get angry, scream
At their round clock faces

Or try to break the glass,
We only hurt ourselves.
The days remain intact.

They wake us up
With light and leave us
In the dark.

For night is not
Their weakness – but a tease
To make us dream of death.

There is no end to days.
Only a cloth laid
Over a birdcage.

Vicki Feaver

UNIT 11
AT WORK

FATHER'S GLOVES

Not garments. A craftsman's armour
Worn to blunt the hooks of pain.
Massive, white asbestos mitts
He brought back from the shipyard
Hang cool by his blowlamp
And his sailmaker's palm.*
In his heart, treasured still,
Scored by remembered cinders,
Lie gauntlets from his dirt-track days
That sometimes, when his fire is dull,
He wears to prod the embers.
Keeping them rekindles him.

He keeps them all, the pairs
We give him on his birthdays,
Crammed in drawers too full to shut.
Some of them may have a use
At family ceremonial:
But, christening or funeral,
Pigskin, suede, kid or calf,
We'd have him carry them, because
His hands are warmer with them off.

Ted Walker

*An instrument used instead of a thimble.

What's in this poem?

Ted Walker's poem combines thoughts on working with the hands, with **memories** about a man's working life.

What does he tell you in the first line about the gloves? Why is the word 'armour' used? Was the armour necessary?

Where did Father work? Try to decide what his **attitude** towards gloves is now. Does he ever wear them?

Is there anything at home that your grandfather or grandmother used in their work? Try to get grandparents to talk about their **experiences** at work. They may have stories about the things that happened to them that you can use in your writing.

Have you ever done a job? Whether it's a paper round, a Saturday job, helping on the market, whatever, write about what you do or have done.

Has anything interesting or unusual happened to you while you have been at work? Have you a relative or neighbour who has an interesting job? Interview them about their work.

Read 'Apprentice Worker' by Jackie on page 70. Imagine that you had to work each day like this. Write a description of a day in your life, as a child labourer in Victorian England.

Talk about people and jobs. Why do people work where they do? Are many jobs boring? What do people think about their jobs? Do they find them interesting? Ask around.

Talk to people who are or have been unemployed. What are their feelings? Do they worry about not getting another job?

Nenthead

The lead long drawn
from the mines
and the miners dead.

Their deserted workings
are left like monuments

where the crag crumbles
and the murmur turns
the stone to sand.

The ghostly trickle
of the stream
has washed away the silt

and a soul
poured into me.

Tom Pickard

Apprentice Worker

Running, up and under,
tired and hungry,
you carry on,
or Samuel Greg will dock your pay.
One penny a week, a lot to them.
But the machinery never stops.
Your heart is running fast,
and your hands cut and sore.
You can't take any more.
At last! The bell rings
for another too-short break.

Jackie

Poem for Merseyside

Listen to the sounds
Machinery moving
Men at work
Listen to the sounds again
Years of silence
Years of despair
Listen to the sounds again
The silt has choked
The ships have gone
Listen to the sounds again
Men determined
Men decided
Listen to the sounds again
The docks will come alive
Their buildings used once more
Listen to the sounds again
Listen to the sounds
Not single seagulls calling now
Not eerie whistling winds
Not silent crumbling buildings
Not empty sludge-filled docks
Listen to the sounds again
Listen to the noise
It's getting louder, louder, louder
It is the sound of LIFE.

Robert and Colin

The Barber Shop

The barber shop has curtains
but it must have been a long time since they were washed
for they are a dark grey
and falling apart;
the window itself is dirty
and whatever signs it has are grey with dust.
The barber stands in the doorway
wearing a coat of uncertain white
over dirty trousers –
and he needs a shave badly.
The shop is called in bold letters
'Sanitary Barber Shop',
and there are those, I suppose, who believe it.

Charles Reznikoff

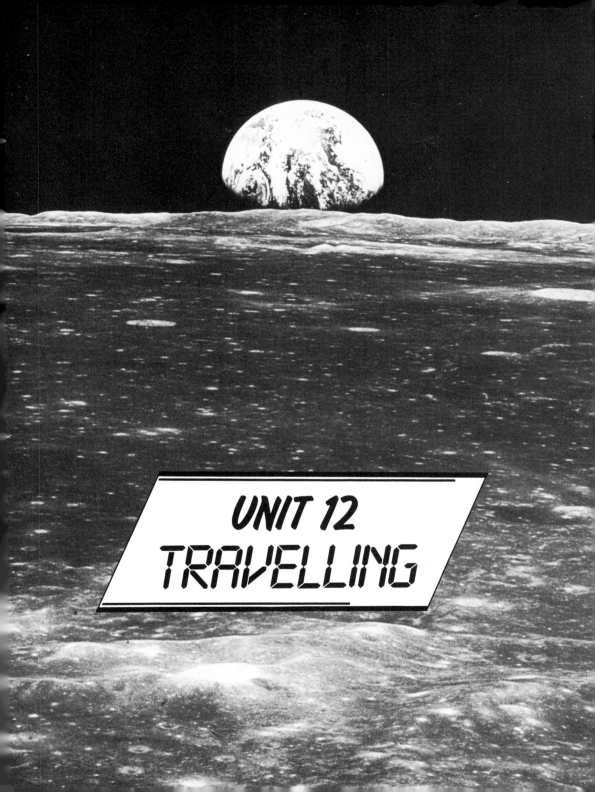

UNIT 12
TRAVELLING

OFF COURSE

the golden flood
the cabin song
the growing beard
the shining rendezvous
the hot spacesuit
the imaginary somersault
the turning continents
the golden lifeline
the crawling deltas
the pitch velvet
the crackling headphone
the turning earth
the cabin sunrise
the shining spacesuit
    the crackling somersault
    the rough moon
    the weightless headphone
    the floating lifeline
    the crawling camera
    the space crumb
    the orbit mouth-organ

the weightless seat
the pitch black
the floating crumb
the orbit wisecrack
the smuggled mouth-organ
the visionary sunrise
the space debris
the space walk
the camera moon
the rough sleep
the space silence
the lifeline continents
the hot flood
the growing moon
    the visionary rendezvous
    the smuggled orbit
    the cabin debris
    the pitch sleep
    the turning silence
    the crackling beard
    the floating song

Edwin Morgan

What's in this poem?

This poem by Edwin Morgan contains a lot of **images.** What are they describing? How many words about space can you find?

Look at the way the words in the poem are set out. Why has the writer **shaped** the poem this way? Why do you think that the poem is 'split' from line 15? What does this tell you?

What words describe the darkness of space?

Talk about the images in the poem with your teacher. Do they help to give you an **impression** of space? Think of other images that describe what you think space must be like.

Space exploration is continuing all the time. What are the newest discoveries and journeys? Think of ways that you can bring these in to your writing.

Why do men explore space? How do you think we will travel in the future?

Many of the lines from the poem would make good titles for other poems. Which ones do you think would be suitable? Lead on into a poem from one of them.

Describe a journey from Earth to a space station. Collect technical space words to include in your writing. Perhaps present your journey in the form of a diary. Include impressions of your life in the capsule, details of your space work, views of the universe outside, your thoughts as you travel. Read your completed 'log' on to the tape.

Read 'Portrait of a Motor Car' on page 78. Look for the images for moving at speed. How would you write a description to show speed of **movement**? Make up some images of your own to give the impression of moving at speed.

Legging the Tunnel

I don't know whether I believe
All Grandpa says:
Whether there ever really was
A tunnel
From side to side
Only an inch or so more wide
Than a canal boat;
Or that
Wrapped in a boatman's duffel coat
He had a ride
Under the Wren's Nest Hill.

The water he said, lay black and still
When they cast off the horse,
And nosed the boat by pole
Into that dark, unwinking hole.

I can remember Grandpa's words:
'Out of a world of sky and trees and birds
We slid;
Out of the yellow sun
Into the rifle barrel of a gun
It seemed;
No path,
Only a tube
Of brickwork half awash with water
Where a shout
Bounced off the rounded, echoing roof
Ridged with worn bands
Of masonry;
Ribbed to the touch of groping hands
Like a knitted sleeve turned inside out.

'Two miles of tunnel
If you snuffed the lantern half-way through
And lost
The capering ogres on the walls
The blackness sucked and blew
In a whistle past you to a pin-hole of light,
The tunnel end.
You were alone
In a pipe of starless night;
Only the slap and chuckle of the water on the sides
As the boatman lay
Shouldering back
On the cabin ramp
And walked the ceiling like a fly
With hob-nailed boots.

'We were
Legging the tunnel.'

Gregory Harrison

Motorway

Like a snake
on a serpent's tongue
carrying cars forward
towards a greedy mouth.

A taxi like a beetle,
red cars like berries.
Only small on the vast space.

Lindsey

Canal

The canal consisted
of floating fuel fluid.
The atmosphere
was heavy
with smoke fumes.

Jane

This Subway Station

This subway station
with its electric lights, pillars of steel, arches of cement,
    and trains –
quite an improvement on the caves of the cavemen;
but, look! on this wall
a primitive drawing.

Charles Reznikoff

Portrait of a Motor Car

It's a lean car . . . a long-legged dog of a car
    a grey ghost eagle car.
The feet of it eat the dirt of a road . . . the wings of it
    eat the hills.

Carl Sandburg

UNIT 13
GAMES

I'LL STAND THE LOT OF YOU

I'll stand the lot of you, I said
to the other kids. They said: Right!

I was Wolves 1957-58:
Finlayson; Stuart, Harris; Slater, Wright, Flowers; Deeley,
    Broadbent, Murray, Mason, Mullen.
The other kids were Rest of the World:
Banks; Pele, Best; Best, Pele, Pele; Best, Pele, Charlton,
    Pele, Best.
Jimmy Murray Kicked off for Wolves.

Wolves were on top in the opening minutes,
then Rest of the World broke away and scored
seven lucky goals. Wolves were in trouble!
But then tragedy struck Rest of the World:
Pele had to go and do their homework!
They were soon followed by Best and Charlton.
It was Wolves versus Banks!
Now Wolves played like a man possessed.
Soon they were on level terms!
Seven-all, and only minutes to go,
when suddenly – sensation! Banks went off
to watch the Cup Final on television!
Seconds later, a pinpoint Mullen centre
found Broadbent completely unmarked
in front of goal. What a chance!

He missed it,
and Wolves trooped sadly off towards their bike.

Martin Hall

What's in this poem?

Martin Hall's poem is an account of a game of street football. Why has the Rest of the World team got five Peles and three George Bests? What caused the problems for the Rest of the World? Who won the game?

Whichever sport we follow, we try to be like our heroes, the 'stars' of that sport. Have you ever played a game like the one described in the poem? Who have you pretended to be? What is your favourite team? If you were to play now, which famous footballer would you be?

Why do people enjoy playing games? Is playing games and sports good for you?

Talk about watching sport. Do spectators get as much enjoyment from the game as the players? Do *you* watch sport on television? What types of sport? Discuss the risks there might be in making your career in sport.

What other sorts of games do you play? Do you play 'imagination' games like that in Richard Hill's 'Cowboy' (page 83)?

Perhaps you have played hide and seek. What happened to the child in Vernon Scannell's poem, 'Hide and Seek'(page 84)? Has this ever happened to you?

Write your own description of an imaginary game. It can be any sport: a football or netball game, a swimming race, a tennis match. You can be any sports star that you want.

Write an account for a newspaper of a game that you have watched or played in.

Describe any unusual sport that you have seen on television. What did you like about it?

Work with your group to design and write a sports magazine. Include reports of games, descriptions of players and teams, a letters page, interviews, crossword, etc.

Listen to commentators describing games on television or the radio. Make your own tape of a commentary of a sports event. Describe the action in detail so that the listener can follow what is happening.

Northern Line

a ten-year-old boy
             with glasses
and scraggy
                 red hair
keeps falling off
           to sleep
he counts
           the cooling ovens
they're all around
                         a forest
    of smoking towers
by him
           a white bag
with blue letters
LEEDS UNITED
           and in gold
THE CHAMPIONS

is that your team?

aye!
      who d'you support
          newcastle?
          I don't suppose you
want to talk about
           last saturday!

I didn't

Tom Pickard

Cowboy

I remember, on a long
Hot, summer, thirsty afternoon
Hiding behind a rock
With Wyatt Earp
(His glasses fastened on with sellotape)

The Sioux were massing for their last attack

We knew

No Seventh Cavalry for us
No bugles blaring in the afternoon
I held my lone star pistol in my hand
Thinking
I was just seven and too young to die
Thinking

Save the last cap
For yourself.

Richard Hill

Hide and Seek

Call out. Call loud: 'I'm ready! Come and find me!'
The sacks in the toolshed smell like the seaside.
They'll never find you in this salty dark,
But be careful that your feet aren't sticking out.
Wiser not to risk another shout.
The floor is cold. They'll probably be searching
The bushes near the swing. Whatever happens
You mustn't sneeze when they come prowling in.
And here they are, whispering at the door;
You've never heard them sound so hushed before.
Don't breathe. Don't move. Stay dumb. Hide in your
   blindness.
They're moving closer, someone stumbles, mutters;
Their words and laughter scuffle, and they're gone.
But don't come out just yet; they'll try the lane
And then the greenhouse and back here again.
They must be thinking that you're very clever,
Getting more puzzled as they search all over.
It seems a long time since they went away.
Your legs are stiff, the cold bites through your coat;
It's time to let them know that you're the winner.
Push off the sacks. Uncurl and stretch. That's better!
Out of the shed and call to them: 'I've won!
Here I am! Come and own up I've caught you!'
The darkening garden watches. Nothing stirs.
The bushes hold their breath; the sun is gone.
Yes, here you are. But where are they who sought you?

Vernon Scannell

UNIT 14
NATURE

THISTLES

Against the rubber tongues of cows and the hoeing
hands of men
Thistles spike the summer air
Or crackle open under a blue-black pressure.

Every one a revengeful burst
Of resurrection, a grasped fistful
Of splintered weapons and Icelandic frost thrust up

From the underground stain of a decayed Viking.
They are like pale hair and the gutturals of dialects.
Everyone manages a plume of blood.

Then they grow grey, like men.
Mown down, it is a feud. Their sons appear,
Stiff with weapons, fighting back over the same ground.

Ted Hughes

Child on Top of a Greenhouse

The wind billowing out the seat of my britches,
My feet crackling splinters of glass and dried putty,
The half-grown chrysanthemums staring up like accusers,
Up through the streaked glass, flashing with sunlight,
A few white clouds all rushing eastward
A line of elms plunging and tossing like horses,
And everyone, everyone pointing up and shouting!

Theodore Roethke

Numbers

A thousand and fifty-one waves
Two hundred and thirty-one seagulls
A cliff of four hundred feet
Three miles of ploughed fields
One house
Four windows look on the waves
Four windows look on the ploughed fields
One skylight looks on the sky
In that skylight's sky is one seagull.

Stevie Smith

UNIT 15
CREATURES

CONSIDERING THE SNAIL

The snail pushes through a green
night, for the grass is heavy
with water and meets over
the bright path he makes, where rain
has darkened the earth's dark. He
moves in a wood of desire,

pale antlers barely stirring
as he hunts. I cannot tell
what power is at work, drenched there
with purpose, knowing nothing.
What is a snail's fury? All
I think is that if later

I parted the blades above
the tunnel and saw the thin
trail of broken white across
litter, I would never have
imagined the slow passion
to the deliberate progress.

Thom Gunn

What's in this poem?

Thom Gunn's poem asks us to 'consider' the snail. He wants us to look closely at the snail. To carefully look at the way it **moves.** The poem contains different words to describe the movement of the snail. How many can you find? **Observe** other creatures and note down movement words for them.

Look at this short poem, which describes the movement of a worm. Notice the movement words and how they build up a clear picture of a slippery worm.

> sleek, smooth,
> slipping and sliding,
> through the mud.

Write short poems of two or three lines to describe the movement of a creature. Some starting points: an ant crossing the floor; a frog in the garden; a cat on the prowl; a wasp in a room. Keep your eyes open for more examples around you.

Thom Gunn describes the snail as 'hunting'. Is this a surprising word to use about a snail? Think of other creatures you might describe as hunters.

What other word does the poet use to make you **compare** the snail with a larger animal? Why does he do this?

Why does the writer use the expression 'a snail's fury'? Invent **phrases** to describe clearly 'feelings' other creatures might have – for example, the rage of an ant.

Imagine that you become a creature. Think about your new physical appearance. How do you **move?** What **size** are you? Where do you find food? Write a description of yourself as this creature.

Try out ideas of **movement** to bring your creature to life. Show your size. Mime your actions.

With your group imitate shapes and movements of other creatures. How would you mime a spider?

from **The Fly**

The fly's sick whining buzz
Appals me as I sit
Alone and quietly,
Reading and hearing it
Banging against the pane,
Bruised, falling, then again
Starting its lariat tour
Round and round my head
Ceiling to wall to floor.

But I equip myself
To send him on his way,
Newspaper clutched in hand
Vigilant, since he may
Settle, shut off his shriek
And there lie mild and weak
Who thirty seconds ago
Drove air and ears mad
With shunting to and fro.

Anthony Thwaite

Rookery

Here they come, freckling the sunset,
The slow big sailers bearing down
On the plantation. They have flown
Their sorties and are now well met.

The upper twigs dip and wobble
With each almost two-point landing,
Then ride to rest. There is nothing
Else to do now, only settle.

But they keep up a guttural chat
As stragglers knock the roost see-saw.
Something's satisfied in that caw.
Who wouldn't come to rest like that?

Seamus Heaney

Creatures

You creatures of the underworld,
slimy, greasy, slippery,
with jade green eyes,
piercing, like arrows,
boring through me
deep into my skin.

You creatures of the underworld,
lumbering, heavy, clumsy,
with long snake-like tails,
slithering along the ground,
and your spiky, humped backs
like a thousand nails standing up,
on a heavy piece of wood.

Suzanne

Horses

Horses stand up still on the skyline,
Waiting for something to happen;
Strangely thoughtful with big sad eyes,
Watching the rain fall mistily,
The clouds move, or just the distance
Escaping from them.
Horses gallop sometimes – up hills,
Across fields, thundering wild,
In a mad explosion of power;
Hot, steaming, violently animal,
But specially, individually horse.
They flail the air and the ground,
Hard-stiff on legs bone-right
And solid-hooved of nail and iron.
They fetlock thrash the tufts of grass and hair,
Rioting down bone and sinew,
Hurrying to be there.
Gigantically gentle with children,
They feel friendly to the touch,
And take sugar quietly.
Stallion-proud and still they look back
To their primeval youth.
They have learnt to be patient.

Paddy Kinsale

FISH

TROUT

Hangs, a fat gun-barrel,
deep under arched bridges
or slips like butter down
the throat of the river.

From depths smooth-skinned as plums
his muzzle gets bull's eye;
picks off grass-seed and moths
that vanish torpedoed.

Where water unravels
over gravel-bed he
is fired from the shallows
white belly reporting

flat; darts like a tracer-
bullet back between stones
and is never burnt out.
A volley of cold blood

ramrodding the current.

Seamus Heaney

What's in this poem?

Seamus Heaney's poem 'Trout' uses different **images** to describe the fish. The power and quality of the images bring the trout to life on the page.

Notice how **comparisons** appear in nearly every line of the poem. How many can you find? List them. What is the trout compared to in the first line of the poem? There are several comparisons with 'firing' or 'shooting'. Find them. Why is this image used?

What expression in the first verse tells you how the trout moves through the water? Find the things he takes from the surface of the water. What is the fish compared to in the way that he does this?

Where can the trout be found?

Do you like the images used to describe the trout? What other images for the trout could you use?

Think of other types of fish. Make up some images to describe them.

Read the extract from Ted Hughes' poem 'Pike' on page 102.

What word would you use to describe the pike? What images describe it? How are the two poems different?

Seamus Heaney captures in words the silent movement of the fish. Make a list of **movement words** for fish. Describe in detail the movement of one kind of fish. Invent images to make your description more vivid.

Read the short poems written by children, in this unit. Write your own, three or four line descriptions of fish.

Four Fish

1. Pike

Still as a stone
This waterlogged log
Lies all alone
Digesting a frog;

But see how the shoals
Of small-fry flinch
As he tilts his scales
At a pound to the inch.

2. Rudd

Swimming as close to the sun as they are able
They turn the afternoon into a fable,
Rolling like gold coins on a miser's table.

3. Tench

This underwater navvy with the blood-shot eye
Is a hard-shovelling mud-lover, black as green can be;
When he's earned his grub, he makes quite a splash,
And his little barbels droop like a Mexican moustache.

4. Perch

Striped like a chunky peppermint humbug,
He gob-stoppers one of his bag of grayling,
Fencing the rest with a threatening shrug
Of a back-fin spiky as an iron railing.

Ted Walker

Fish

Eyes staring
Searching around the sea,
Camouflage
When its enemy appears.

Ann

Pike

A luminous body
Sabotaging in the reeds.
A submarine swerving
to avoid the dazzling bait.

Karl

Fish

The inquisitive creatures
   submerge, looking for
some findings on the sea bed.

Una

Polluted Stream

Dead fish slithering
like tiny vessels
blown out of the water.

Philip

from **Pike**

Pike, three inches long, perfect
Pike in all parts, green tigering the gold.
Killers from the egg: the malevolent aged grin.
They dance on the surface among the flies.

Or move, stunned by their own grandeur,
Over a bed of emerald, silhouette
Of submarine delicacy and horror.
A hundred feet long in their world.

In ponds, under the heat-struck lily pads –
Gloom of their stillness:
Logged on last year's black leaves, watching upwards.
Or hung in an amber cavern of weeds.

The jaws' hooked clamp and fangs
Not to be changed at this date;
A life subdued to its instrument;
The gills kneading quietly, and the pectorals.

Ted Hughes

UNIT 17
CRUELTY !

THE DOG LOVERS

So they bought you
And kept you in a
Very good home
Central heating
TV
A deep freeze
A very good home –
No one to take you
For that lovely long run –
But otherwise
'A very good home'
They fed you Pal and Chum
But not that lovely long run,
Until, mad with energy and boredom
You escaped – and ran and ran and ran
Under a car.
Today they will cry for you –
Tomorrow they will buy another dog.

Spike Milligan

What's in this poem?

Spike Milligan's poem offers some thoughts on animal suffering. Often, as in this poem, the owners' cruelty may not be deliberate, but caused by people not knowing how to look after their pet properly.

What sort of home did the dog have? Name the important thing it did not have. Why did it need to get out?

Why did the people buy the dog in the first place? Did they care for the dog? Do you think they will buy another one?

Do you keep a pet? Does it get enough exercise? Talk about whether the owners described in 'Dog Lovers' should be allowed to have a dog. How can they be prevented from having one, or mistreating it?

Do you care about what happened to the dog in the poem? Would you care if it happened in your neighbourhood? Discuss what you could do about it.

Do you think that pet shops should sell dogs without checking up on buyers first? Think of a time of year that often sees cases of cruelty.

Why do dog owners choose 'Pal' and 'Chum' dog foods? How do they know these are good for their dog?

Make up a name for a new dog food. Design a poster to advertise it. Don't forget a slogan to help sell it.

Write a short television commercial (about 60 seconds) to promote your product. Write a short catchy 'jingle' for it (four lines is enough).

Write your own poem, warning people to take care of their pets.

Take One Home for the Kiddies

On shallow straw, in shadeless glass,
Huddled by empty bowls, they sleep;
No dark, no damp, no earth, no grass –
Mam, get us one of them to keep.

Living toys are something novel,
But it soon wears off somehow.
Fetch the shoe-box, fetch the shovel –
Mam, we're playing funerals now.

Philip Larkin

Goldfish

the scene of the crime
was a goldfish bowl
goldfish were kept
in the bowl at the time:

that was the scene
and that was the crime

Alan Jackson

My Mother Saw a Dancing Bear

My mother saw a dancing bear
By the schoolyard, a day in June.
The keeper stood with chain and bar
And whistle pipe, and played a tune.

And bruin lifted up its head
And lifted up its dusty feet,
And all the children laughed to see
It caper in the summer heat.

They watched as for the Queen it died.
They watched it march. They watched it halt.
They heard the keeper as he cried,
'Now, roly-poly!' 'Somersault!'

And then my mother said, there came
The keeper with a begging-cup,
The bear with a burning coat of fur,
Shaming the laughter to a stop.

They paid a penny for the dance,
But what they saw was not the show;
Only, in bruin's aching eyes,
Far-distant forests, and the snow.

Charles Causley

UNIT 18
WEATHER

BLUE TOBOGGANS

scarves for the apaches
wet gloves for the snowballs
whoops for white clouds
and blue toboggans

stamping for a tingle
lamps for four o'clock
steamed glass for buses
and blue toboggans

tuning-fork for Wenceslas
white fogs for Prestwick
mince pies for the Eventides
and blue toboggans

TV for the lonely
a long haul for heaven
a shilling for the gas
and blue toboggans

Edwin Morgan

What's in this poem?

How many words or expressions in this poem make you think of winter? How do the children keep warm in the snow? Count the different activities mentioned in the poem. What are the 'lonely' doing?

Why is the phrase 'and blue toboggans' repeated at the end of each verse?

What kind of scene do you imagine when you read the poem? Do the **images** in the poem form a picture?

Talk about how winter affects you. What games do you play in the snow? What is it like walking to school in winter? How does the weather affect older people? Think which people have to go and work outside, despite the weather.

Ask people what they most like and dislike about winter weather.

List the **sights** and **sounds** that you associate with winter. Form these into sets of lines that give you a clear picture of winter. Use images that describe the **feelings** of cold and the **sights** of the season.

What does a tree look like in winter? Describe its shape, movement, colours, appearance.

Write, from your own experience, about an incident involving winter weather. Use short descriptive sentences to show how the weather affected the experience.

In groups, act out playing in the snow. For example, mime the movements of a snowball fight. What movements does a skater make on ice?

Mime other actions in the snow for your group to guess. What different types of weather can you show by mime?

Wind

This house has been far out at sea all night,
The woods crashing through darkness, the booming hills,
Winds stampeding the fields under the window
Floundering black astride and blinding wet

Till day rose; then under an orange sky
The hills had new places, and wind wielded
Blade-light, luminous black and emerald,
Flexing like the lens of a mad eye.

At noon I scaled along the house-side as far as
The coal-house door. I dared once to look up –
Through the brunt wind that dented the balls of my eyes
The tent of the hills drummed and strained its guyrope,

The fields quivering, the skyline a grimace,
At any second to bang and vanish with a flap:
The wind flung a magpie away and a black-
Back gull bent like an iron bar slowly. The house

Rang like some fine green goblet in the note
That any second would shatter it. Now deep
In chairs, in front of the great fire, we grip
Our hearts and cannot entertain book, thought,

Or each other. We watch the fire blazing,
And feel the roots of the house move, but sit on,
Seeing the window tremble to come in,
Hearing the stones cry out under the horizons.

Ted Hughes

Rain

Rain
When it falls on land
Is a strange element, owned
By gutters and ponds and pools;
Welcome, yet other,
To buds whose wheels it greases,
Mineral, yet not quite brother,
To dust and stone and sand.
On land we keep account of rain
By watching clouds and hearing the drip in the eaves
And knowing the smell of it among the leaves.
But rain
When it falls on sea
Is scarcely seen or heard or smelt
But only felt –
As if a skelter of birds with pittering feet
Were lighting on the glass roof of the waves.
The unsalt water falling through the passive air
Has not identity there
Where each drop tastes of the full Atlantic brine.
Back again in the sea
Rain
Is only sea again.

Norman Nicholson

Winter

A frost-bitten ground,
Plants stark dead
In the frozen earth,
Snow-whipped trees
Bow in the icy wind,
Famished birds whirl through
The half-solid sky.

Chris

Rainfall

The rain pounding across the road
racing from the sky.

Michael

Winter's Day

Biting cold,
the influence of the air,
deep depression soaks you.

James

WHAT'S IN A POEM?
Description

Read 'Child on Top of a Greenhouse' by Theodore Roethke on page 89.

The poem **describes** an incident, a child stuck on the roof of a greenhouse. The action has stopped and the poem captures one moment in time. This piece of writing shows the likeness between a poet and a photographer. A photographer takes a **visual picture** of a scene. He or she shows all the details. Here, the writer has described in words exactly what is happening in the scene. He has made a detailed **word picture** of what he can see. The word picture is so clear that we can see the incident just as if we had been there.

This is only a short poem, but the poet has made each word work. Each line gives an important piece of detail to the reader.

Look at the poem again and see how much you are being told. What is the wind like? Pick out the details we are given about the boy. Describe how he feels. What is in the greenhouse? What is the weather like? Are you told the type of trees? Notice what they look like. Did anyone see the incident?

Quite a lot of information for a seven line poem! The writer has not wasted a word. He has used each word like the piece of a jigsaw. Each one is important in building up the complete picture.

Write what you think will happen next in the poem. Continue in the same style, making each word work for you.

Have you ever been in an unusual situation? Write down what you remember about it. In your notes try to collect as many actual facts as you can. Work from your notes to write your descriptive poem of the incident. Use the form of one complete thought or statement on each line.

Shape

ring
clatter
ding dong
peal chime

pins points needles prickles sharp spines
snuffles snorts
curling
rolling
ball

Look at the **shape poems** above. Each poem is made up of words about the object, arranged in a shape to look like it. Collect **adjectives** (describing words) about each of the following objects. Arrange the words from your list to make them into the shape of the object.

diamond   aeroplane   butterfly   balloon   ghost

Collect words to describe the movements of a cat. Arrange the words into the shape of a cat. Also collect words to describe the movements of a snake, a fish, a tortoise, a worm. Arrange the words to make the shape of the creature.

kroweriFirework

The shape
of a volcano
the glowing lava
comes out and covers
the ground in colours.

This is Philip's firework poem. He wrote a poem about a firework and then he arranged the words and lines of the poem into the shape of a firework.

Write short poems to describe these things:

snowflake   giraffe   ship   mouse   kite

Now arrange the words of your poems to make the shape of their titles. See if you can make simple shape poems about other animals or objects.

Look at the two examples of shape poems below. What are the poems about? How are they different from the other examples on the page? Try to make up other shape poems of your own.

FRUSTRATION

FRustrAtIOn   NOItartSurF
RUstFraTION   NOITar FtsUr
FRUSTraTion   NoiTarT Surf
NoitartSURF   RUSTfatrION
FRUSTRATION
RFUstTrAion
SRFutRTIaoN
FFrrrRR uuUSStTrraAAttTiilooONNn
FrRUSsttrRATiilooOnnNN
FfrustTrAtIIiOOnN
nOITArTSurF
OINtraUtsFr
FrrrRssUU tt RRR ttt TIil OonNNN
TTTTT UUUUU
aassoooiinn
SFRUtartOInnIOtratURFS
NFIsruTtaoN   NOaTturslfN

Neil

WAR

war
raw
red   w   ar
m   wnswa   rrr
r   aw   sn   e   m
purplewa   r
dr   y   wa   r
words   war
warwor   ds
warwarwarwarwarwarawrawrawrawrawraw
m   ens   war   purplew   ar   re
d   wa   r   me   ns   purpl
e   r   ed   raw   war
war   war   war   war   war   *Neil*

Experiences

Read 'Hide and Seek' by Vernon Scannell on page 84.

'Hide and Seek' describes an **experience** shared by many of us. How did this particular game end? How did the child feel? Have you ever been left like this? Where did you hide?

Describe another game that you play. How do you play the game? Why do you enjoy it? Write about one good or bad experience you have had while playing the game.

Read 'An Ordinary Day' by Norman MacCaig on page 39.

The writer notices even the most 'ordinary' things. He shows us that if we look, if we observe, what is happening around us, we will never be short of things to write about. We share experiences every minute of every day – if we notice them!

What 'ordinary' things are mentioned in the poem? Keep your eyes open. Note down the simple things that you see. Try to write short poems about your own 'ordinary days'.

Read the extract from 'The Fly' by Anthony Thwaite on page 94.

Subjects for writing are all around. You are sitting, waiting for something interesting to write about. Nothing is happening. Suddenly, a buzzing sound announces the arrival of a fly to pester you. Anthony Thwaite's poem captures the incident. How does he get rid of the pest?

Imagine you are sitting alone in a room. What disturbs you? Is it a noise? What happens next?

Moods

Read 'Horses' by Paddy Kinsale on page 96.

The writer gives three very different pictures of horses in the poem. He describes horses in three different **moods**.

Look at lines 1 to 6. How are the horses described? What is their mood? Which word best describes it?

In lines 7 – 17, the horses are described very differently. What are they doing? Which words show their mood?

In lines 18 – 23 of the poem, how are the horses described? What adjectives best describe their mood?

Which mood of the horses do you like best? Can you think of other animals you could describe in this way? Write a short descriptive poem to show an animal in its different moods.

Read the extract from 'Blackberry-picking' by Seamus Heaney on page 60.

What mood was the child in while blackberry-picking? What makes you think so? Pick out the words or expressions that tell you whether he enjoyed it. What did the blackberries taste like? What mood do you think the child was in at the end of the poem? Why?

Read 'Dumb Insolence' by Adrian Mitchell on page 6.

What mood is the boy in? Pick out the words that tell you how he is feeling. Why do you think he feels this way? Have you ever felt like this? Describe how you behaved.

Write two poems describing yourself, one in a good mood and one in a bad mood. Explain how you felt and why. Choose your words carefully to describe each mood.

Comparisons

Read 'Wind' by Ted Hughes on page 112.

Look at how the poet describes the wind. How does he make the wind come to life? He uses **comparisons**. For an example, look at lines 15 and 16. This description of the gull is a comparison. The writer is telling us that the wind is so strong that it could bend an iron bar. There are many comparisons in the poem. They make the poet's description more powerful and effective.

Look at the poem closely. What picture do you see? How strong do you think the wind is? Which comparisons tell you this?

Some of the comparisons are introduced by the word 'like'. These are called **direct comparisons**. Find them in the poem.

Not all comparisons need the word 'like', but the writer is still comparing one thing with another. Find examples of this in the poem. Look at the first line. How is this a comparison? What are the foundations of the house compared to in the last verse?

Comparisons help a writer to give us a clear description. They help our imaginations to see more clearly the picture that the writer is giving us.

Read 'November Night, Edinburgh' by Norman MacCaig, on page 27.

The comparison in the first line immediately tells you what kind of night it is. How many other comparisons can you find in the poem?

What does the writer compare the fog to? Look for the clue in line 4. Why is the world 'a bear shrugged in his den' (line 13)?

Think of comparisons which would describe clearly: a storm; a river flowing; winter; pop music; a painting. Collect images which describe types of weather: rough seas; stormy nights; dark nights.

Arrange the images and comparisons into lines of **free verse** to describe clearly each subject.

Movement

Read 'Portrait of a Motor Car' by Carl Sandburg, on page 78.

How does the poem give you the **impression** of speed? Pick out the words or expressions that suggest that the car is moving quickly.

What other words describe the **movement** of a car? Use these words to describe a car speeding along a motorway.

Compare your ideas with 'Motorway' by Lindsey on page 77. How does she see the cars moving along the motorway? What does she compare them with?

Read 'Legging the Tunnel' by Gregory Harrison on page 76.

What sort of movement is the writer describing? Find the movement words in the poem.

What difference is there in the **pace** of the poem from that of 'Portrait of a Motor Car'? Why is this? Does the pace of each poem make it more effective?

What other words could describe movement on water?

Read 'The Boxer' by Lynn, on page 33.

What movement words does Lynn use to describe the boxer? What other words could she have used?

List other sports. Write movement words to describe the actions needed for each sport. Now write a poem about your favourite sport, using movement words from your list to describe playing it.

ACKNOWLEDGEMENTS

Photographs

The editor and publishers would like to thank the following for permission to reproduce photographs: David Richardson for pages 7, 8, 23, 26, 29, 33, 38, 40, 44, 47, 51, 52, 61, 65, 67, 95, 107, 113, 114. Network Photographers (Mike Abrahams) for page 15. Les Baker for page 55. BBC Hulton Picture Library for picture 70. Science Photo Library for page 73. Frank Lane for pages 85, 91, 97, 102. Sue Ainley for page 103.

Text

We would like to thank these authors and their agents for permission to print the following material:

'Fish and Chips' by L T Baynton from *Have You Heard The Sun Singing?* (Evans Brothers). 'Number 14' from *Stations* by Keith Bosley (Anvil Press Poetry 1979) ©Keith Bosley. 'Notes for the Future from *A Single Flower* by Jim Burns. 'My Mother Saw a Dancing Bear' from *Collected Poems* by Charles Causley (Macmillan). 'I Wonder How Many People in this City' from *Selected Poems 1956-68* by Leonard Cohen (Jonathan Cape Ltd). 'Home' by Paul Donnelly from *Smoke* Magazine. 'Arithmetic' from *The Deceptive Grin of the Gravel Porters* by Gavin Ewart (London Magazine Editions) ©Gavin Ewart. 'Days', 'Round Pond' and 'Slow Reader' by Vicki Feaver ©Vicki Feaver. 'City Lights' by Margaret Greaves from *Your Turn Next* (Methuen Children's Books). 'Nearly Thirteen' and 'Writing' by Jan Dean ©Jan Dean. 'Considering the Snail' reprinted by permission of Faber and Faber Ltd from *My Sad Captains* by Thom Gunn. 'I'll Stand the Lot of You' by Martin Hall from *Strictly Private* (Kestrel Books). 'Legging the Tunnel' ©Gregory Harrison reprinted by permission of the author from *A Second Poetry Book* published Oxford University Press. 'Blackberry Picking' and 'Trout' reprinted by permission of Faber and Faber Ltd from *Death of a Naturalist* by Seamus Heaney; 'Rookery' from *Bulls Eyes* by Seamus Heaney (Longman 1977/ Faber and Faber Ltd. 'Cowboy' by Richard Hill ©the Author. 'A Boy's Head' and 'History Lesson' from *Miroslav Holub: Selected Poems*, trans Ina Milner and George Theiner (Penguin Modern European Poets 1967) pp 54, 72, ©Miroslav Holub 1967. Translation ©Penguin Books, 1967. Reprinted by permission of Penguin Books Ltd. 'Thistles', 'Pike' and 'Wind' reprinted by permission of Faber and Faber Ltd from *Wodwo, Lupercal* and *Hawk in the Rain* by Ted Hughes. 'Goldfish' ©Alan Jackson. 'Horses' by Paddy Kinsale from *Thoughtshapes* ed. Barry Maybury (Oxford University Press). 'Take One Home for the Kiddies' reprinted by permission of Faber and Faber Ltd from *The Whitsun Weddings* by Philip Larkin. 'Talk' from *The Complete Poems of D H Lawrence* (William Heinemann Ltd) reprinted by permission of Laurence Pollinger Ltd and the Estate of Frieda Lawrence Ravagli. 'The Man Who Wasn't There' from *Late Home* by Brian Lee (Kestrel Books 1976) pp 29-30 ©1976 by Brian Lee. Reprinted by permission of Penguin Books Ltd. 'School Poem' by Brian McCabe from *Strictly Private* (Kestrel). 'November Night, Edinburgh' and 'An Ordinary Day' from *The Sinai Sort* and *Surroundings* by Norman MacCaig (The Hogarth Press Ltd). 'Café Portraits' by Roger McGough from *Penguin Modern Poets 10* (*The Mersey Sound*) reprinted by permission of A D Peters & Co Ltd; 'The Lake' from *Holiday on Death Row* by Roger McGough (Jonathan Cape Ltd). 'The Dog Lovers' by Spike Milligan, from *Small Dreams of a Scorpion* (Michael Joseph). 'Dumb Insolence ©Adrian Mitchell appeared in *For Beauty Douglas* (Collected Poems 1953-1979) (Allison and Busby, 1982). 'The Apple's Song', 'Blue Toboggans' and 'Off Course' from *From Glasgow to Saturn* by Edwin Morgan (Carcanet Press). 'Rain' reprinted by permission of Faber and Faber Ltd from *The Pot Geranium* by Norman Nicholson. 'Street Boy' from *Salford Road* by Gareth Owen (Kestrel